SS521-AJ-PRO-010

0910-LP-107-2826

Revision 1

Guidance For Diving In Contaminated Waters

PUBLISHED BY DIRECTION OF COMMANDER, NAVAL SEA SYSTEMS COMMAND

15 March 2008

LIST OF EFFECTIVE PAGES

Date of issue for original is:

Original .... 15 March 2008

TOTAL NUMBER OF PAGES IN THIS PUBLICATION IS 36, CONSISTING OF THE FOLLOWING:

*Zero in this column indicates an original page.

A

NAVSEA TECHNICAL MANUAL CERTIFICATION SHEET

Certification Applies to: New Manual ☐   Revision ☒   Change ☐

Applicable TMINS/Pub. No.   SS521-AJ-PRO-010

Publication Date (Da, Mo, Yr) 15 March 2008

Title: GUIDANCE FOR DIVING IN CONTAMINATED WATERS

_____

_____

TMCR/TMSR/Specification No.: _____

CHANGES AND REVISIONS:

Purpose: Update procedures for diving in contaminated waters. _____

_____

_____

_____

Equipment Alteration Numbers Incorporated: _____

TMDER/CAN Number Incorporated: _____

Continue on reverse side or add pages as needed.

CERTIFICATION STATEMENT

This is to certify that responsible NAVSEA activities have reviewed the above identified documentate for acquisition compliance, technical coverage, and printing quality. This form is for internal NAVSEA management use only, and does not imply contractual approval or acceptance of the technical manual by the Government, nor relieve the contractor of any responsibility for delivering the technical manual in accordance with the contract requirement.

Authority	Name	Signature	Organization	Code	Date
Acquisition	LT J. Pearson		NAVSEA	00C38	3/12/08
Technical	R. Whaley		NAVSEA	00C3	3/12/08
Printing Release					

This page is left blank intentionally.

RECORD OF CHANGES

CHANGE NO.	DATE OF CHANGE	TITLE AND/OR BRIEF DESCRIPTION	ENTERED BY

This page is left blank intentionally.

Table of Contents

Safety Summary

GENERAL SAFETY

This Safety Summary contains all specific WARNINGS and CAUTIONS appearing elsewhere in this manual and are referenced by page number. Should situations arise that are not covered by the general and specific safety precautions, the Commanding Officer or other authority will issue orders, as deemed necessary, to cover the situation.

SAFETY GUIDELINES

Extensive guidance for safety can be found in the OPNAV 5100 series instruction manual, Navy Safety Precautions.

SAFETY PRECAUTIONS

The WARNINGS, CAUTIONS, and NOTES contained in this manual are defined as follows:

WARNING Identifies an operating or maintenance procedure, practice, condition, or statement, which, if not strictly observed, could result in injury to or death of personnel.

CAUTION Identifies an operating or maintenance procedure, practice, condition, or statement, which, if not strictly observed, could result in damage to or destruction of equipment or loss of mission effectiveness, or long-term health hazard to personnel.

NOTE An essential operating or maintenance procedure, condition, or statement, which must be highlighted.

. WARNING During surface decompression operations, incomplete decontamination of Divers may contaminate recompression chambers and present a fire hazard. (Page 4-2)

WARNING The MK 21 helmet is not suitable for use in CAT 1 diving. Testing at NEDU confirms there is a risk of some water or vapor ingress into the MK 21 Helmet. (Page 4-3)

CAUTION Any breach of personal protective equipment used to conduct a dive in contaminated water should result in termination of the dive as soon as possible to limit exposure to the hazards. (Page 4-7)

This page is left blank intentionally.

CHAPTER 1

Introduction, Scope, And Purpose

1.1 INTRODUCTION

Contaminated water is defined as water which contains any chemical, biological, or radioactive substance which poses a chronic or acute health risk to exposed personnel. Some degree of contamination and/or pollution is evident in practically every body of water in the world. The contamination may be naturally occurring or come from a variety of sources including terrorist acts, leaking vessels, industrial discharges and/or sewer effluent. However, much of the contamination that enters the water is not readily apparent. The biggest concern is from relatively enclosed bodies of water, such as lakes, rivers, or harbors which are within close proximity to large populations and wrecks, where contamination can accumulate and/or concentrate.

These contaminants could present a potential health risk to Navy Divers and may additionally impact mission and operational readiness. The effects on personnel may become evident immediately (acute) or may be delayed for many years (chronic) especially in the case of exposures to carcinogenic substances. For most microbiological exposure, illness will not develop for several hours after diving and could possibly be delayed for days. With the exception of chemical/biological warfare agents, acute toxicity and/or incapacitation is unexpected for most chemical exposures. However, chronic sub-toxic exposure to a variety of chemical hazards may affect illnesses such as cancer, neurodegenerative disease, hormonal disregulation and others.

1-1.1   **Purpose**. The purpose of this manual is to provide general guidance and basic procedures for diving in contaminated water. Because of the wide variability in contaminants, potential exposure levels and other variables, only general guidance can be provided. Supervisory personnel are encouraged to contact local agencies to obtain information on local water contaminants and hazards.

1-1.2   **Standard Military Syntax.** This manual utilizes standard military syntax as pertains to permissive, advisory, and mandatory language. Word usage and intended meaning in this manual is as follows:

a. "Shall" has been used only when application of a procedure is mandatory.

b. "Should" has been used only when application of a procedure is recommended.

c. "May" and "need not" have been used only when application of a procedure is discretionary.

d. "Will" has been used only to indicate futurity; never to indicate any degree of requirement for application of a procedure.

This page is left blank intentionally.

CHAPTER 2
Contaminants And Hazards

2-1 GENERAL

The three types of contaminants Divers can expect to encounter are chemical, biological, and radiological. The potential routes of exposure for Divers are inhalation, ingestion, absorption, and impingement (forcing of material into the body, such as through a wound). Unless the response is to a specific incident, the availability of quantitative data on the contaminants present in any specific body of water is problematic. Real-time, or even near real-time, water analysis is not currently feasible. If a specific contaminant is suspected, information from various sources is available such as Material Safety Data Sheets (MSDS), shipping manifests, or sampling and analysis.

2-2 CONTAMINANTS AND HAZARDS

Biological contaminants come from humans and animals, urban and industrial sewage, marine and fresh water organisms, commercial ships, hazardous waste sites, marinas, and agricultural runoff. The main source of biological contaminants in water is human sewage. The environmental fate of most pathogens in water is unknown. It is prudent to assume water bodies contain the microbiological organisms of diseases present in a local population unless confidence is high in the effectiveness of the local wastewater treatment facilities. Such confidence is unjustified in underdeveloped areas and even in CONUS after an unusually heavy rainfall. Biological agents are divided into two broad categories, pathogens and toxins.

NOTE   **Both Chemical And Biological Contaminants Tend To Concentrate In Sediment Rather Than In The Water Column.**

2-2.1   **PATHOGENS.** Pathogens are infectious agents that cause disease in man, animals, or plants. These include bacteria, viruses, and parasites. These are commonly referred to as germs. While the vast majority of microorganisms are harmless or even helpful, there are many naturally occurring pathogens which are harmful to humans. Pathogens cause disease (infection) by entering the body through lungs, digestive tract, and the skin and mucous membranes of body openings. Once they enter the body pathogens multiply, overcoming the body's natural defenses, and produce disease. Symptoms most commonly associated with pathogen infection include upper respiratory flu or cold like symptoms, vomiting, diarrhea, pneumonia, or skin lesions. Some pathogens cause nervous system damage such as headache, paralysis, convulsions, or coma.

Viruses are the smallest of the all biological agents able to reproduce. They are incapable of independent life, since they are only genetic material (DNA or RNA) and some encapsulating proteins. They can be dangerous when they enter a human cell, and "hijack" the contents to reproduce themselves. Smallpox and influenza are examples of viruses. Viruses are difficult to detect, and most hospital laboratories are not equipped to do so routinely. Viruses are difficult to treat after exposure, since they are not susceptible to common drugs. Some virus protection can be gained by prior immunization, e.g., Hepatitis A; but no vaccines exist for most viruses.

Bacteria are living microorganisms. Unlike viruses and rickettsias, they are capable of reproduction outside living cells. If they enter the body and if the victim is not properly treated, the microorganism will multiply and incapacitate the host. Bacteria can be found in almost any environment. Eschericia coli (E. coli) is a well known bacteria which is commonly associated with contamination of processed meat products. Some strains of E. coli are common inhabitants of the human intestine, and thus are used as an indicator of human feces and to open/close public beaches. Examples of diseases caused by bacteria are cholera and anthrax. Seawater is estimated to contain up to a million bacteria per cubic centimeter. Bacteria sometimes concentrate in a thin layer on the water surface, or a thin layer on the top of sediment.

"Parasites are single-celled or multi-celled organisms that live and feed on or in another animal. Well-known examples of human parasites are malaria and tapeworms. Most parasites are acquired by ingestion (such as eating raw meat) but some can gain entry into humans by skin contact either on land or in the water. Most water dwelling parasites that can cause disease in humans are found in tropical fresh water (as found in Central and South America and Southeast Asia). Salt water parasites rarely cause more than a rash and itching. Still, when working in areas where parasites are known to exist, contact can be prevented or minimized in most cases by wearing protective clothing (wet suit or some form of coverall are usually adequate) and bathing soon after surfacing."

2-2.2   **TOXINS.** Toxins are poisonous substances produced by microorganisms (pathogens), plants, or some animals. Some toxins can be chemically synthesized or artificially produced with genetic engineering techniques. Toxins exert their lethal or incapacitating effects by interfering with certain cell and tissue functions. Neurotoxins disrupt nerve impulses while cytotoxins destroy cells by disrupting cell respiration or metabolism. There is a vast range of signs and symptoms associated with toxin exposure which makes diagnosis extremely difficult.

Algal blooms, such as those responsible for "Red Tide," produce toxins which are released into the water. Not all harmful algal blooms (HABs) are red - some are yellow, green and orange. These toxins can cause illness such as cognitive impairment as well as gastrointestinal, respiratory, and dermal distress. Algal outbreaks of human concern are usually associated with large fish kills. Common symptoms one might experience when exposed to these toxins are coughing, eye and skin irritation, runny nose, numbness around the mouth, and nausea.

2-2.3   **Blood Borne Pathogens**. Though many of these pathogens are viruses they are addressed separately since they are generally passed from person to person through direct contact with an infected person's body fluids. These infectious blood borne diseases, e.g., HIV and hepatitis, are most likely to occur when an operation involves the recovery of human remains. Divers may also be exposed through inadvertent contact with potentially infected material such as hypodermic needles or open cuts. Most known infectious agents pose a minimal risk to Divers since the agents are fragile and do not survive long outside a host. The Hepatitis C virus is less fragile, but infectivity in underwater recovery situations is expected to be low. Divers should complete the series of the standard immunizations required for healthcare workers, including those for Hepatitis A and B virus as well as tetanus. Personnel should be trained in exposure control and safe handling of potential infected material, similar to the training recommended for healthcare workers. Besides the immediate medical concerns, the fatigue and mental health issues associated with the recovery of human remains should be considered as part of operational planning.

2-3 INDUSTRIAL TOXIC/CHEMICAL CONTAMINANTS AND HAZARDS

Based on the number of Material Safety Data Sheets now available, it appears that more than 5,000,000 chemicals are in commercial use worldwide. Chemicals vary widely in availability, solubility, toxicity, and permeability. Generally, as it relates to diving, little to no information is available on either the acute, or chronic toxicity of these chemicals, or their environmental fate. Again the primary sources of industrial chemical contamination are industrial spills, urban and industrial sewage, commercial ships, hazardous waste sites, and agricultural runoff. It is expected that every body of water in the world is contaminated to some degree. The National Institute of Occupational Safety and Health (NIOSH) publishes a handbook which lists the exposure criteria for approximately 1,500 of the most common chemicals for which a health hazard analysis has been completed. The guide is available for download at http://www.cdc.gov/niosh/npg/. The website also lists contact information to obtain hard copies or a copy on CD ROM for a minimal fee. If the presence of a specific chemical is confirmed, some information may be available to assess the risk. The following paragraphs are a general list of chemicals which Divers can expect to encounter.

2-3.1 **HYDROCARBONS.** Hydrocarbons are chemicals composed essentially of atoms of hydrogen and carbon. They range from small and light substances (natural gas) to large and hard to evaporate molecules (coal). In between are a range of solvents, oils, fuels, and the larger polyaromatic hydrocarbons (PAHs). PAHs are about the heaviest hydrocarbons able to evaporate and able to dissolve in water. All the common hydrocarbons are in fact complicated mixtures of chemicals, and will have different compositions in different locations at different times. Even MIL-SPEC diesel fuel, hydraulic oil, and creosote are all complicated hydrocarbon mixtures (with lots of PAHs) having no full chemical specification. Creosote, commonly used as a wood preservative, is a petroleum derivative that contains PAHs and is a known carcinogen. The amount of creosote leaching into adjacent water decreases with time; newer pilings, dock supports, etc. may pose a greater health risk than those in place for several years.

2-3.2 **HEAVY METALS.** Metals in purified form are solids with low potential of being toxic; unfortunately, they are not usually encountered in purified forms. Metals combined with other chemicals can form stable minerals that also have low toxicity. In the marine environment, metals can also exist as dissolved ions, adsorbed into other solids like clay or humus, or chemically combined into an organic compound, such as methyl mercury. Many water quality limits on metals are based on dissolved ions, as that form is considered to carry the greatest hazard to fish. Consistent with that assumption, the usual tests for metals in water initially convert all forms into metal ions.

2-3.3 **POLYCHLORINATED BIPHENYLS (PCBs):** PCBs are materials that were used as paint additives and electrical equipment coolants. PCBs were banned from production and use in 1977 in North America for concern over health effects associated with them. PCBs do not readily decompose and have been discovered in the sediment of many bodies of water. OPNAV Instruction 5100.23 addresses Navy occupational exposure to PCBs. Chloracne is a severe skin condition associated with exposure to PCBs. Prolonged dermal exposure to PCBs is a significant health concern.

2-4 CHEMICAL/BIOLOGICAL WARFARE AGENTS

Chemical/Biological warfare agents present an extreme hazard to a Diver and every attempt should be made to identify the agent and mitigate the concentration/exposure prior to diving. The U.S. Army Field Manual (FM) 3-9 Potential Military Chemical/ Biological Agents And Compounds has information on the chemical makeup and characteristics of specific agents and should be used as the initial reference source if tasked to respond to an incident involving a chemical or biological warfare agent. Distribution of FM 3-9 is limited to military and government agencies. However, it does not contain specific information on the environmental fate of these compounds in sea water. Other available sources of information are other military field and technical manuals, e.g., FM 3-5 NBC Decontamination and the Chemical and Biological Information and Analysis Center (CBIAC): Tel: (410) 676-9030 Fax: (410) 676-9703, web address: http://www.cbiac.apgea.army.mil/

2-5 RADIOLOGICAL CONTAMINANTS AND HAZARDS

Divers may respond to an emergency situation where the diving area is contaminated with a radiation source, or may be required to perform inspection, repair or maintenance in the fuel pools of nuclear power reactors. Radiological contamination is most likely occur through an accident or intentional terrorist act. All Divers must have a thermo luminescent dosimeter (TLD) or similar item, and be told of the locations of radioactive items. Nuclear shipyard Divers are experienced and trained in diving near point sources of radiation. Diving within the fuel pools of nuclear power reactors is done internationally by civilian contractors working for private or government-operated power companies.

CHAPTER 3
Equipment

3-1   GENERAL

There is no single equipment configuration or material which will protect the Diver under all conditions or from all contaminants. The type of protection needed will be determined by the expected hazard, type of work, the urgency of the work, and the available equipment. The diving support system should include both respiratory and physical protection. The standby Diver must be equipped with a level of protection at least equal to that worn by the Divers. Additionally, the surface tenders and support personnel may experience as great a hazard as the Diver. The mucous membranes are the most vulnerable regions on the body and, assuming intact skin, are essentially the only route microorganisms can enter and infect the body. Therefore, isolating these vital areas from the source of contamination is the primary concern when diving in a biologically contaminated environment. Respiratory and physical protection must be available for surface support personnel.

3-2   SCUBA EQUIPMENT

Diving with a standard SCUBA ensemble including a half face mask and a mouthpiece regulator provides very little protection to a Diver. The Diver's mouth is in constant contact with the water exposing the Diver to contaminants which can enter either around the mouthpiece or via water refluxed through the exhaust valve. Inhalation of microscopic water droplets from the area of the regulator mouthpiece and from its exhaust valve may cause contamination to go to the lungs and on to the bloodstream. SCUBA is not to be used for diving in Category (CAT) 1, 2 or 3 contaminated water. (See Table 4-1 for categories and definitions.)

3-2.1   **FULL FACE MASK.** If the primary hazard is microbial, a full-face mask may reasonably protect mucous membranes in the eyes, nose, and mouth. Both NOAA and the EPA use a full-face mask for contaminated water diving. An obvious advantage in using this approach is the portability and relative ease of use of a full-face mask. Full-face masks can be configured to operate with compressed gas SCUBA tanks, a configuration that affords a Diver unencumbered freedom of movement and provides moderate protection. Most full-face masks can also be configured to operate from surface-supplied compressed gas which affords greater endurance but restricts mobility compared to SCUBA. A recent international diving survey found no commercial diving operations using full-face masks for contaminated water diving. A full face mask which incorporates a positive-pressure regulator will help eliminate water entering the mouth, but does not resolve the droplet inhalation concern. Additionally, full-face masks offer no protection for the Diver's head, neck, or ears, all of which are potential sites for exposure to waterborne hazards.

3-2.2   **CLOSED/SEMI-CLOSED CIRCUIT REBREATHERS.** Using a full face mask with a rebreather, such as the MK 16 or MK 25, would mitigate exposure through exhaust valve reflux and allow for complete encapsulation of a Diver in a protective over suit. Accordingly, in some scenarios use of these apparatus should be considered.

3-3   SURFACE SUPPLY DIVING SYSTEMS

3-3.1   **MK 20.** The MK 20 offers an added level of protection over half-masks and mouthpiece regulators. Operating the MK 20 in the positive-pressure mode will lessen the likelihood of water leaking into the mask. However, some water is likely to enter either under a poor-fitting face seal or as reflux through the exhaust valve. Therefore, the MK 20 and other full-face masks are not to be used in CAT 1 or 2 contaminated water.

3-3.2   **MK 21 Diving Helmets.** By sequestering the Diver from the water column the MK 21 surface supplied hard hat equipped with the double exhaust kit, when mated to a vulcanized dry suit offers a good level of protection for Divers in contaminated water making it suitable for CAT 2 CWD when a KM37 (NS) helmet is not available. Unlike masks, the MK 21 is able to protect a Diver's entire head, including his ears. However a problem frequently reported with the MK 21 is reflux of water through the exhaust valve mechanism. Even when outfitted with the double exhaust kit for diving in contaminated water, some water occasionally leaks back into the helmet. This allows some water to accumulate in the oral/nasal mask portion of the helmet so that when the Diver triggers the demand regulator with his next breath, he aspirates and/or ingests an atomized spray of water containing contaminants from the water column making the MK 21 unsuitable for use in CAT 1 contaminated water diving (CWD). This problem is most often reported in water with high particulate matter content such as suspended silt and sediment. For the MK 21, leakage of water into the helmet can be mitigated by adjusting the dial-a-breath to a slight free-flow when the Diver reaches the bottom to effect a slight positive pressure.

Another concern reported with the MK 21 occurs during use in water heavily contaminated with petroleum products. The exhaust whiskers of the double exhaust kit are manufactured from a dipped latex procedure, and are highly susceptible to degradation by petroleum products, as well as many other solvents. They will require frequent replacement to maintain the integrity of the helmet. Some operators have had to perform annual maintenance procedures on the MK 21 daily while diving in such environments. Ample supplies of spare parts including o-rings and double exhaust kits should be available when preparing to dive in water contaminated with petroleum-based materials. NAVSEA is currently pursuing replacement of these soft goods with more resilient materials. Leakage into the oral nasal mask will occur at any depth when the head is moved from the upright position. Leakage can be minimized by opening the steady flow slightly. Adjusting the dial-a-breath has no influence on whether or not leakage occurs.

3-3.3   **KM 37 (NS) Diving Helmets.** The KM 37 (NS) offers all the benefits of a MK 21 as detailed above but in addition it is equipped with a quadruple exhaust valve thus reducing the likelihood of reflux of water through the exhaust valve mechanism. This makes the helmet the preferred helmet for use, over the MK 21, in Cat 2 CWD. In addition the KM 37 (NS) forms the base helmet for use with the Regulated Surface Exhaust modification system currently under development and designed for use in CAT 1 CWD.

3-3.4 **Umbilicals.** Standard Divers' air supply hose is comprised of nitrile with a neoprene outer shell. This combination is reasonably resistant to many chemicals. However, prolonged exposure to concentrated chemical contaminants, especially solvents, may lead to decomposition of the hose. Careful inspection of hoses is warranted before and after diving in contaminated water.

3-4 DIVING DRESS

The type of diving dress selected will be based upon several considerations such as the water temperature, level of contamination, and type of contaminant. No suit can protect a Diver from all substances, however a dry suit with attached gloves connected to a positive surface supplied helmet is the best protection for a Diver in contaminated water. Coated exterior fabric dry suits may be difficult to decontaminate. Some contaminants may cause such rapid deterioration of material, or may be so difficult to clean from the diving dress, that a new suit and other equipment may be needed for each dive. This increase in required equipment should be included in planning operations. The type of dress chosen should have strength, flexibility, ease of decontamination, and, most importantly, chemical resistance. It should preclude any contact between the human body and the contaminants.

3-4.1 **WET SUITS.** Wet suits offer little to no protection while diving in certain levels of contaminated water. The skin is directly exposed to the contaminants in the water while foam neoprene can absorb large amounts of contaminated water making decontamination difficult. In addition some contaminants can degrade foam neoprene. Wet suits are not appropriate when diving in CAT 1 or 2 contaminated waters.

3-4.2 **DRY SUITS.** Dry suits, either variable or constant volume, are appropriate for diving operations in contaminated water. A one-piece dry suit is preferred with the goal of minimizing the number of penetrations. Vulcanized dry suits offer substantial protection from all microbiological hazards and from many chemical hazards for extended periods of time. The Viking HD, should be used for all diving in CAT 1 or 2 contaminated water. The dry suit should have a neck dam that creates a watertight seal directly to the MK 21 or KM 37 (NS). Intact skin is susceptible to many hazards including PAHs (in high concentrations in petroleum products), PCBs, pesticides, creosote, and some heavy metals. Isolating a Diver in a dry suit is highly recommended when these materials are present. Divers may experience some leakage of water if a suit is not properly fitted. Care should be taken to ensure Divers and dry suits are matched appropriately by size.

Viking and Gates publish data for resistance of their respective suits to a host of chemicals. When concentrations of known contaminants are available this information should be referenced for maximum safe dwell times. Consideration of the durability of other components of the diving ensemble, such as the helmet, gloves, umbilical etc., should be taken into account when determining dwell times. Evidence a suit is being degraded by contaminants are swelling of the material, color changes, tackiness, stiffness when dry, and exposure of underlying fabric. Suits demonstrating any of these changes should not be reused.

3-4.3   **TESTING DRY SUIT.** Prior to using a Drysuit for CAT 1 or CAT 2 CWD the suit should be tested for leaks. To do this the neck and cuffs must be sealed. This can be achieved by using suitably sized bottles, balls or if available custom built bungs, the cuffs should be sealed using the dry gloves that will be used for the dive. The suit should then be inflated and either covered with soapy water, a 'snoop' liquid or submersed in clean water in order to detect any leaks. Obviously a leaky suit should not be used for CWD.

3-4.4   **GLOVES.** Chemically resistant waterproof gloves should be used when diving in contaminated water. Gloves should be positioned over cuff rings on the sleeves of the Viking HD dry suit. Depending on the nature of the diving job, an over-glove may be used to protect against chafing and punctures. In cold water, thermal under-gloves may be necessary. For extra security, gloves should be taped or zip tied to the dry suit sleeve above the cuff ring. Gloves should not be equalized with dry suits to minimize the possibility of contamination entering the entire suit in the event of a tear.

3-4.5   **OVERSUITS.** If it is reasonable to expect to encounter bulky, adherent contaminants during a dive, a disposable oversuit, e.g., TYVEX®, may be used. Such disposable hazardous material protective suits can be secured to a Diver after he has been outfitted with the entire diving rig. No effort to make the oversuit watertight should be attempted, for such an attempt may complicate the dive by creating air pockets.

3-5 COMPRESSORS

A concern for conducting diving operations in contaminated water is compressed gas supply. Since compressors are often used on site to compress gas as needed, volatilized components of waterborne hazards can potentially enter an on-site compressor and contaminate the gas supply. Historically, the primary source of contaminated air samples has been from compressor intakes not being positioned upwind or away from the source of contamination, e.g., fuel oils, hydrocarbons. Operations supervisors, therefore, should be careful to position compressor intakes upwind of contamination, if possible. Such optimal positioning may not always be feasible or reliable, so compressing gas off the site may be a prudent alternative and may mitigate the chances of contaminants entering Diver gas supplies.

CHAPTER 4

Pre-dive Planning

4-1 GENERAL

NOTE   **Prior to conducting diving in Category (CAT) 1 contaminated water, diving supervisors should contact SEA 00C3 for support in obtaining information on potential levels of contamination, specific procedures, and local support agencies.**

The majority of U.S. Navy diving will occur in water with few obvious signs of contamination. In the dive planning stage, operational risk management (ORM) techniques (OPNAVINST 3500.39A) should be used to balance the risks of an operation against the potential risks to personnel and equipment. The potential routes of exposure for Divers and topside personnel to chemical/biological contamination are inhalation, ingestion, absorption, and impingement. A good risk assessment will identify the expected route(s) of exposure, expected contaminant(s) and reasonable precautions necessary to minimize the exposure to both the Diver and topside personnel.

Most chemical hazards to which Divers are exposed cause limited immediate effects. For most microbiological exposures, illnesses will develop hours to days after exposure. However, chronic exposure to chemical hazards may cause/effect the occurrence of other illnesses such as cancer. Recognition and identification of substances is of paramount importance if adequate and appropriate monitoring of exposed personnel is to be conducted by medical authorities.

Diving in water heavily contaminated with pathogenic microbes may infect an otherwise seemingly innocuous skin wound. For this reason, Divers with preexisting, unhealed wounds should be prevented from diving in contaminated water. Any injuries that they sustain during such diving should require them to exit the water for immediate medical attention.

The expected decompression obligation and decontamination procedures to be implemented should be thoroughly briefed to the dive team during the planning phase. Diving in CAT 1 or 2 contaminated water should be scheduled to require no in-water decompression in order to limit the Diver's exposure to waterborne hazards. Decontamination and Diver undress procedures, within the five-minute time constraint, should be demonstrated to the Diving Officer before attempting dives relying on surface decompression. As described in the decontamination section, decontamination procedures are tedious and may require a prolonged time. Every effort must be taken to ensure thorough decontamination is achieved prior to recompressing Divers because introducing contaminants to recompression chambers may present significant health and safety concerns.

WARNING During surface decompression operations, incomplete decontamination of Divers may contaminate recompression chambers and present a fire hazard.

4-2 MEASUREMENT AND MONITORING

Reliable analysis of water for chemical and microbiological substances is difficult to obtain. Simply sending the water sample "to the lab" will not give a complete picture of the contaminants present. Most laboratory techniques are not designed to scan for all possible contaminants at once, but rather must be focused narrowly to provide optimum results. Analysis of a water sample for the potential 5,000,000 chemical contaminants is impracticable. Microbiological testing requires entirely different analytical methods than those which detect chemical contaminants. The scope of testing should be limited by prior research of local conditions and concerns. There is also usually a 2 or 3 day lag between sampling and reporting. Tests are available which cover more than one substance, such as 8 metals, or 11 PAHs, at once, for about $100 per sample.

Additionally, depending on the nature of a contaminant, it may float on the surface, suspend in the water column, or accumulate on the bottom. An accurate analysis requires samples throughout the entire water column and adjacent sediment. The validity of samples collected is also likely to be dependent on several other variables which change over time including current, tide, temperature, and weather. The variation in contamination across space and time is simply unknown. For these reasons, real or near-real time water analysis is not currently feasible.

Generally, only a qualitative water quality assessment is possible since a complete and reliable analysis of the contaminants present in the water is difficult, if not impossible, to obtain. Supervisors should obtain as much quantitative information as possible to aid in their assessment. This information may be available from various sources including local water quality management offices, contained in environmental studies or available from local environmental regulation agencies. If a specific contaminant or hazard is suspected, sampling and analysis should be completed prior to commencement of dive operations. The risk assessment should be thorough in order to best protect the Diver and topside personnel. Several of the factors that should be considered in this analysis are the nature of the contamination, urgency of the required operations, the natural environmental, type of body of water, and the diving and protective equipment available.

4-3 LEVELS OF PROTECTION

Based upon the expected primary source of contamination, the protective ensemble chosen should minimize the exposure route. With the exception of CAT 1 the following are the levels of protective equipment, associated with each category of contaminated water, currently available on the ANU list.

4-3.1   **Category 1.** Grossly contaminated water and extreme risk of injury (even death) to unprotected divers. Divers must be fully encapsulated with a diving helmet using a surface exhaust or positive pressure free flow helmet.

NOTE   **Prior to any CAT 1 diving, commands shall contact NAVSEA for advice on diving procedure and the supply of any necessary protective equipment. NAVSEA will detail any exposure time limits on a case by case basis depending on the contaminant and based on the latest research available.**

With oil based contamination, it is likely that silicone components will be the first to fail (see 4-3.2). NAVSEA is working to provide replacement components that will last for hours rather than minutes in such environments. Breakthrough times are also available for Viking Dry Suits.

All CAT 1 diving equipment shall be tested for leaks and damage prior to diving (see para 3-4.3). Diving Commands shall maintain logs for all diving life support equipment (LSE) exposed to CAT 1 contamination to include exposure times and details of the contaminant to which it was exposed to enable calculations of exposure times for future dives.

4-3.1.1 **Category 1 Dress:**

a. Viking Heavy Duty Vulcanized Rubber dry suit with attached boots and neck dam.

b. Dry gloves attached with cuff ring. Tape and/or outer locking rings shall be used to ensure seal. Inner chemical protection gloves shall also be worn.

c. Diving Helmet. NAVSEA is working with industry to develop a bolt-on surface exhaust system for the KM 37 (NS) which will provide a surface exhaust capability that will greatly reduce the risk of contamination entering the helmet. The system also includes modifications for the dump valve on the heavy duty Viking Dry Suit which connects to the surface exhaust system thus fully encapsulating the diver. If a requirement to dive in CAT 1 water occurs prior to the introduction of this system, then NAVSEA will provide the diving system to be used.

WARNING   The MK 21 helmet is not suitable for use in CAT 1 diving. Testing at NEDU confirms there is a risk of some water or vapor ingress into the MK 21 Helmet.

When a diver is fully encapsulated, overheating can rapidly become a problem if diving in warm water. A number of commercial systems are being developed. Traditional cooling systems are unsuitable for use during contaminated water diving (CWD) as they use surface supplied water which not only introduces more protential points of failure to the suit but also runs the risk of the surface supply becoming contaminated. Current best practice is to provide gel pack cooling vests or ice vests and to limit the duration of the dive. It is also vitally important that all divers and tenders remain well hydrated.

Topside Dress will need to be tailored to meet the specific risks of the dive. It may also be possible to reduce topside dress protection to Level C as detailed by OSHA Standard 29 CFR 1910.120 APPENDX B. Level C is comparable with current MOPP4 Chemical Warfare Suits and protective masks. A link to OSHA 29 CFR 1910.120 APPENDIX B is available on the SUPSALV CWD webpage http://www.supsalv.org/00C3_CONWATER.ASP. Note that airborne substances must be known and monitored and that Level C will not protect against toxic industrial chemicals (TIC). Normally for CAT 1 dives Level B protection will be required consisting of a non-encapsulating, chemical-resistant suit, often called a splash suit and self-contained breathing apparatus, worn either inside or outside the suit. In some CAT 1 environments it may be necessary for topside personnel to adopt Level A (tender is fully encapsulated) protection. Topside dress requirements will be decided by the onsite commander in consultation with NAVSEA until more permanent procedures are issued.

4-3.2   **Category 2.** Heavily contaminated water with a high risk of injury to unprotected divers. Divers must be fully encapsulated with diving helmet (helmet may exhaust to water).

Exposure times for CAT 2 diving will be dependent upon the local situation. However, if diving in particularly concentrated oil based contamination, or other volatile chemical, then dives longer than 22 minutes involve increased risk. Recent testing has shown that Jet A Fuel will cause a catastrophic failure of existing Kirby Morgan Helmet diaphragms and O-Rings in around 22 minutes (testing involved 100% concentrations of Jet A Fuel and such concentrations are highly unlikely outside of the laboratory).

The diving supervisor may extend the duration of the dive for operational reasons if satisfied that concentrations of contaminants are low enough to justify the extended exposure. If required to dive in a tank or other similar small, contained body of water with high concentrations of oil based contaminants, or other corrosive material, then NAVSEA should be contacted as it may constitute a CAT 1 dive. Chemical distortion and weakening of the materials used in suit and helmet manufacture is a cumulative process therefore equipment used in CWD must be inspected more closely than other diving equipment and the following maintenance actions are to be conducted daily on equipment used for CAT 2 CWD:

a.   Mission Maintenance Procedures Appendix A-5 of MK-21
Technical Manual. MK 21 MIP Control Number 5921/162 Periodicity Code R-1, R-2, R-3, and if conditions warrant a complete 24M-1R.

b.   Viking Dry Suit MIP Control Number 5921/174 Periodicity Code
R-1, R-2.

c.   KM 37 MIP Control Number 5921/163 Periodicity Code R-1, R-2, R-3, and if conditions warrant a complete A-1R.

To prove the integrity of the diving equipment prior to any CAT 2 dive, in addition to any routine inspection dry suits should undergo a full leak test (see para 3-4.3).

4-3.2.1 **Category 2 Dress**:

a. Viking Heavy Duty Vulcanized Rubber Dry Suit with attached boots and neck dam.

b. Dry Gloves attached with cuff ring. Tape and/or outer locking rings should be used to ensure a seal. Inner chemical protection gloves should also be worn.

c. Diving Helmet. KM 37 (NS) helmet is the most suitable ANU helmet for CAT 2 CWD. It should always be used in preference to MK 21 as NEDU testing indicates there is a small ingress of water and vapor into the MK 21 helmet via the exhaust valve. The quadruple exhaust valve on the KM 37 (NS) is believed to reduce, but not eliminate, this ingress, particularly if a head up attitude is maintained. Further testing of the KM 37 (NS) is scheduled to validate performance. Topside personnel will also require protection and should be provided with skin protection in the form of a Tyvek, or other similar, suit (available commercially) and rubber gloves (meeting OSHA Standard 29 CFR 1910.120 APPENDX B requirements). To protect the face from splash hazards, a perspex face shield should be used and, at the bare minimum, protective glasses must be worn. It is likely that tenders will not require the respiratory protection normally associated with OSHA Standard 29 CFR 1910.120 APPENDX B Level C dress however, it may be necessary to wear an oral-nasal mask to protect against strong vapor.

As was done for CAT 1 protection, diver and tender overheating must be considered.

4-3.3   **Category 3. Moderately contaminated water with some risk of injury especially if ingested.**

There are no additional procedures for diving in CAT 3 water over and above those contained in the U.S. Navy Diving Manual.

4-3.3.1 **Category 3 Dress:**

Whether diving SCUBA, rebreathers or surface supply a minimum of a full face mask is required in CAT 3 CWD. If diving in an AGA style UBA it is preferable to use it in the positive pressure mode. This will increase the protection offered to the diver from contaminated water.

The level of skin protection is not presently mandated for CAT 3 diving but ORM principles must be followed to decide which level of diving dress is most appropriate. If diving on the hull of a vessel, then a number of risks exist from abrasion hazards (e.g. barnacles) to the risk posed by special paints used on some ship hulls. A long sleeved wetsuit coupled with gloves and a neoprene hood, or in some circumstances coveralls, should be considered if there is deemed to be such a risk.

4-3.4   **Category 4.** Baseline contamination such as EPA's geometric mean levels for E Coli and Enterococci or EU bathing water of 'sufficient' or better. There are no additional procedures for CAT 4 diving and dress is in accordance with the US Navy Diving Manual.

TABLE 4-1. CONTAMINATED WATER CATEGORIES AND DEFINITIONS.

Contaminated Water Categories	Definitions	Previous Categories (for comparison)
CAT 1	a. Grossly contaminated b. Extreme Risk of Injury (or even death) (Note 1) c. Fully encapsulated Diver (inc. Surface Exhaust) (Note 2)	N/A
CAT 2	a. Heavily contaminated b. High Risk of Injury (Note 3) c. Fully encapsulated Diver (in water exhaust) (Note 2) (Note 4)	CAT 1
CAT 3	a. Moderately contaminated b. Some risk of Injury (especially if ingested) c. Full face mask (skin covered as necessary) (Note 5)	CAT 2 and 3
CAT 4	a. Baseline contamination (EU Bathing Water 'Sufficient' or better) b. Low risk of Injury (Note 6) c. Standard diving dress	CAT 4

Notes:

1. Diving is not recommended in CAT 1 environments and only properly qualified and equipped diving teams should dive CAT 1. The diving task must be mission essential and the dive team must have express approval from their Commanding Officer for the dive.

2. Fully encapsulated means a vulcanized rubber dry suit (or other CWD approved dry suit) with integrated boots mated to dry glove with ring system. In addition gloves must be taped and/or clamped to the suit. Equalization tubes between glove and cuff must not be used.

3. Injuries may be major or minor and could include such things as skin irritations, rashes, eye or sinus irritation etc.

4. In water exhaust must be at minimum a double exhaust (e.g. Mk 21) but quadruple exhaust (e.g. KM37 (NS)) should be used if available.

5. Positive Pressure whenever practicable.

6. Low risk refers only to risk from contaminants and does not relate to any other aspect of the dive. A full risk analysis is still required.

CAUTION   Any breach of personal protective equipment used to conduct a dive in contaminated water should result in termination of the dive as soon as possible to limit exposure to the hazards.

4-4   DETERMINING WATER QUALITY CATEGORIES

CAT 1 diving is very uncommon and unless faced with a major incident or highly unusual and specialized diving task it is unlikely that many Divers will ever encounter CAT 1 waters in their careers. CAT 2 water is more common and can be encountered in some industrial diving conditions or following accidents involving chemicals or oils. Much of the operational day to day diving will fall under CAT 3 where there is some biological risk and precautions should be taken to avoid ingesting the water. The level of skin protection for a CAT 3 dive will be dependent upon the dive location. If there is a risk of skin abrasion or irritation then some form of wetsuit or coverall may be appropriate. It is permissible to dive without a wetsuit or coveralls in a CAT 3 environment if the only risk is from ingestion of water. CAT 4 diving will relate to training diving in fresh water and water that is either:

a.   Used frequently (monthly or more often) and known not to pose a risk to our Divers and there has been no recent environmental events (see para 4-5) likely to increase the level of contamination.

b.   Has undergone laboratory or field laboratory testing for water contaminants and is free from harmful contaminants, Or; can be declared free from contaminants by a suitable local authority e.g. harbor master, EPA, Coastguard, NOAA etc.

c.   The dive is in open water, at least 400 yards away from any river or pipeline outfall, harbor mouth, or other inland waterway.

d.   If in doubt or if diving in unfamiliar inland waterways or lakes for which there is no testing data or suitable local knowledge available, then it must be assumed that the water is not CAT 4 and a suitable level of protection adopted.

Until a suitable decision making matrix or field evaluation test kit can be developed, and not withstanding the rules regarding CAT 4 diving above, the decision on which category of contaminated water is appropriate and the associated diving dress remains at the discretion of the dive supervisor. Supervisors are reminded of the need to contact 00C3 if CAT 1 contamination is suspected.

4-5   SPECIFIC DIVING SCENARIOS

Certain scenarios can increase the potential exposure to chemical/biological contamination and extra protective measures should be adopted:

4-5.1   **After Rainfall.** After appreciable rainfall, land-based contaminants may be washed into a watershed basin with the runoff. This phenomenon has been termed "first flush." Dives planned during, or in the days immediately following, a large rainfall should anticipate exposure to a variety of chemical and microbiological hazards when diving in an area with a reasonable expectation of "first flush" effects.

4-5.2   **Working in Sediment.** Most persistent contaminants with a density greater than water will accumulate in the sediment. Of the analysis of water that has been reported, the sediment routinely has significantly higher levels of both chemical and microbiological contamination than the adjacent water column. This contamination may include heavy metals and PCBs.

4-5.3   **Points of Discharge.** Water adjacent to points of discharge such as drainage pipes and runoff channels can contain increased levels of contamination.

4-5.4   **Human Remains Recovery.** For Divers and body handlers in the water, every effort should be made to protect personnel from injury and unnecessary exposure to body fluids and tissue. If the recovery is to be made around wreckage where there is a reasonable concern for injury, Divers should wear reinforced gloves to minimize the chance of introduction of potentially infectious materials to their hands.

4-6   SOURCES OF INFORMATION

Information about water quality may be obtained from state and local health agencies. These organizations often have water testing and reporting procedures in place and are often accessible via the Internet. This information usually focuses on microbiological contamination for recreational waters or fishing estuaries, and is available for most coastal states. For OCONUS operations, the Armed Forces Medical Intelligence Center (AFMIC) can provide some information regarding local water quality. Such information may require a few weeks to compile. Requests should be initiated accordingly. Internet availability to AFMIC can be found at: http://mic.afmic.detrick.army.mil.

4-7   PERSONNEL QUALIFICATIONS / TRAINING

Training is as important as personnel selection. A training program should thoroughly explain contaminants and their properties, precautions, effects of exposure, methods of protection, and emergency procedures. Continuous refresher retraining is imperative to ensure Divers remain competent in the procedures and use of equipment. Depending on the type of toxic substance encountered, it may be advisable to introduce short or long term biological and medical surveillance of exposed personnel.

CHAPTER 5

DIVE STATION DECONTAMINATION PROCEDURES

5-1 DECONTAMINATION

The aim of decontamination is to either rapidly and effectively render contamination harmless or remove it. The goal of systematic decontamination procedures is to limit the spread of the contamination and reduce the levels to the greatest extent possible in order to protect personnel and equipment. The decontamination and monitoring process is unique to each accident/incident. Decontamination techniques may be both physical and chemical. The decontamination methods selected should be tailored to the hazard, responders on scene, location, and equipment available. The tasks performed do not change significantly between different types of contamination but the procedures may vary depending on the nature of the accident/incident and the available equipment. Standard DOD decontamination procedures, as described in various manuals or instructions, e.g., U.S. Army FM 3-5 NBC Decontamination, can be effectively modified to work in diving scenarios. Familiarization and platform specific contaminated water diving drills should be conducted routinely. Such drills should encompass all aspects of diving in contaminated water including equipment selection, donning protective equipment, and decontamination procedures.

NOTE: **Until tests have been completed on various commercial off the shelf decontamination solutions for category (CAT)1 contaminated water diving (cwd), NAVSEA 00C will provide tailored decontamination guidance prior to any CAT 1 dive being conducted.**

5-2 TOPSIDE PROTECTION

Tenders and other topside personnel may also require protection from hazards while supporting diving operations in contaminated water. A thorough hazard analysis will address the degree of protection required by topside personnel as well as the Divers. Every effort should be made to position the "dive station" outside the contaminated area with a transition zone between the work area and the "dive station." Some degree of contamination of the deck and topside equipment will occur and it is expected the umbilicals and line tenders will come into intimate contact with contaminated water and must be appropriately protected. Depending on the nature of the hazard, topside protection may involve the use of splash protection and face shields, impermeable rainsuits, cartridge respirators, disposable hazardous materials suits or a combination of all of the above. For human remains recovery missions, all body handlers should observe universal medical precautions and avoid unnecessary contact with potentially infectious material. All personnel should wear coveralls, thick disposable gloves, and protective eyewear. The same immunization recommendations for Divers apply to tenders. In warm weather, thermal stress can be a severe problem for personnel wearing protective dress. Close monitoring and short rotations of duty may be necessary. Industrial hygiene support from the local military treatment facility, preventive medicine unit, or the Navy Environmental Health Center (NEHC) should be consulted for guidance on the necessity of respiratory protection for topside personnel.

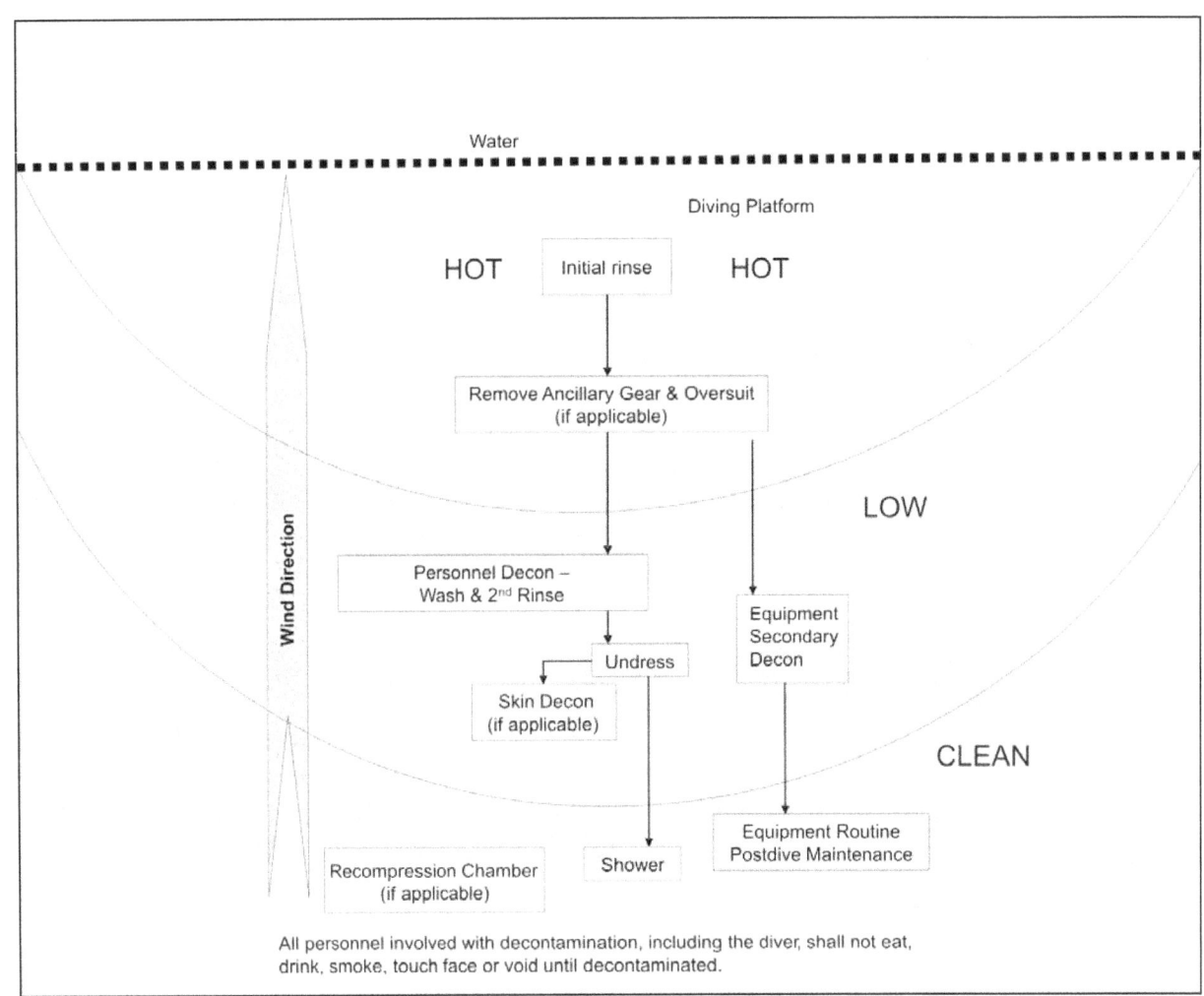

FIGURE 5 - 1 DECONTAMINATION STATION OVERVIEW

5-3 DECONTAMINATION STATION OVERVIEW

Even before diving operations in contaminated water begin, the dive site should be divided into three zones for proper sequestration of contamination throughout the operations, see Figure 5-1. A zone immediately surrounding the point of water entry/exit must be deemed one of high contamination and is referred to as the 'hot zone'. The zone to which Divers and gear progress after completing their initial decontamination following a successful dive is one of low contamination and is referred to as the 'warm zone'. A final zone into which Divers progress after they have been decontaminated and had all their diving equipment removed is known as the 'clean zone'. If feasible, the clean zone should be positioned upwind from the contaminated zones. Positioning of topside personnel may need to be adjusted to keep from spreading contamination.

5-3.1   INITIAL DECONTAMINATION

The initial decontamination step is to spray bulk contaminants off a Diver with a high-pressure, clean, fresh water rinse. Use salt water if fresh water is unavailable. In some circumstances, all fluid used to rinse, wash, and re-rinse the Diver and equipment needs to be captured for appropriate disposal as hazardous material. In such instances, the decontamination procedure needs to be altered. The Diver should not be initially rinsed until he is within a water-impermeable capturing area. Such an area could include sheeting placed on the ground to contain liquids, or a child's wading pool. After all decontamination procedures have been completed, all rinse fluids should be pumped or poured out of this capturing area and into appropriate storage and transport containers for proper disposal. If no effluent needs to be captured, the Diver should be sprayed as he initially exits the water to limit the quantity of contaminants being transferred to the dive station.

Attending technicians should be careful to direct water flow away from potential points of leakage (exhaust valves, seal junctions, etc.) in the Diver's rig: a high-pressure jet of water directed at such potential breach points may inject contaminants inside the protective gear and into contact with the Diver. Tenders should also exercise care that overspray does not spread contamination. Care should also be taken to remove the bulk of contaminants at this stage to ensure the greatest effectiveness of subsequent decontamination steps.

WARNING   A high pressure rinse is not to be used during CAT 1 decontamination due to the increased risk of breaching the diver's personal protective equipment.

5-3.2   INITIAL EQUIPMENT REMOVAL AND WASHDOWN

As the Diver arrives on the dive station following his mission, his oversuit (if applicable) should be cut away to decontaminate the diving rig. This could also be an appropriate time to remove ancillary dive gear such as harnesses, weight belts, emergency gas supply tanks, etc. for subsequent decontamination.

After the Diver has been initially rinsed and his ancillary gear and any oversuit removed, the Diver should be scrubbed with a stiff-bristle synthetic brush and a cleaning solution. The composition of the cleaning solution should be appropriate for the contaminant to be removed; 5% bleach solutions are adequate for most situations and should not degrade equipment when used for short periods of time and then rinsed away. Commercially available household bleach is usually approximately 5%. Table 5-1 should be used when deciding on which decontamination solution is most appropriate. Sometimes a combination of solutions must be used e.g. initial scrub down with Simple Green for oily contamination followed by bleach followed by potable water.

For further advice on decontamination solutions see the EPA Environmental Response Team document 'Diver Decontamination Solutions' available on the SUPSALV website:
http://www.supsalv.org/pdf/DIVER%20DECONTAMINATION%20SOLUTIONS.pdf

Table 5-1 EPA Environmental Response Team - Decontamination Solution Effectiveness/Safety

Decontamination Solution	Use against Biological Contaminants	Use against Chemical Contaminants	Safety for Diver Skin Contact	Dive Gear Compatibility
Potable Water	C	C	1	1
Antimicrobial Soap	A	A	1	1
Bleach	A	B	2	3
Betadine	A	C	2	2
Simple Green	B	B	1	1
Quaternary Ammonium	A	B	3	2
TSP	B	A	3	3
Alcohol	A	C	3	2
	Effectiveness: A = Very Effective B = Effective C = Somewhat Effective		**Safety/Compatibility:** 1 = Not Harmful 2 = Potentially Harmful 3 = Harmful if other precautions are not followed	

Notes:

1. This list is not all-inclusive. Other suitable decontamination solutions may be used at the dive supervisor's discretion.

2. Effectiveness includes both contaminant removal and neutralization.

3. Safety includes both physical harm to the Diver and degradation/staining of equipment.

4. Dive gear compatibility is generalized based on normal decontamination solution concentrations and common dive gear materials. It is recommended that specific gear manufacturers be contacted to determine compatibility.

5. Mention of trade names does not imply product endorsement.

5-3.3   UNDRESS

After the Diver has been adequately decontaminated and moved into the 'warm zone' adjacent to the clean zone, the dive gear should be removed in a stepwise fashion. First, the locking mechanism from helmet to dry suit should be disconnected and the helmet removed. Then the dry suit and gloves should be removed. Next, dive gear undergarments should be removed. If nothing indicates that the diving rig has been breached during the dive, the Diver may proceed to the "clean" zone and take a routine postdive shower, which should include washing of the entire body with soap/shampoo. Diver should use Domboro solution in each ear for a minimum of 60 seconds per side. Additionally, the area under each fingernail should be thoroughly scrubbed with soap and a nailbrush. The Diver should use antiseptic mouthwash to rinse his mouth. If there are indications of possible dermal exposure to contaminants, then additional decontamination steps will be required.

This includes scrubbing the bare skin with a 0.5% bleach solution for approximately 10 minutes and then washing with soap in a shower. The 0.5% solution can be prepared from a 1:9 dilution of the equipment decontamination solution already prepared. Label solutions carefully as applying 5% directly to a Diver's skin can be very irritating. Care should be taken not to introduce decontamination solution into abdominal or central nervous system wounds, if present.

All the Diver's equipment must undergo secondary decontamination after it has been removed from him during the personnel decontamination procedure. This secondary decontamination procedure entails first rinsing bulk contamination from the equipment, then soaking it in a bleach-based solution for at least thirty minutes before actively scrubbing the equipment with soft bristle brushes. Drums or wading pools may be effective repositories for this process. After soaking and scrubbing, equipment should be rinsed thoroughly until no foaming occurs.

Soaking umbilicals in bleach based solutions is not recommended. An alternative solution such as TSP or soap such as Simple Green should be used to thoroughly clean umbilicals. Impermeable covers should be applied to avoid introducing cleaning solutions into the interior of diving umbilicals and other air-handling apparatus.

5-3.4   TENDER DECONTAMINATION
The tender decontamination procedure is the same as that for Divers. The last person out of the contaminated zone will have to self decontaminate.

5-4   MEDICAL SUPPORT

After completing a thorough decontamination, individuals should proceed to a medical evaluation station, if appropriate to the hazard. The individuals' vital signs are taken, documented, and compared with the baseline information. Supervisory personnel will be required to make a differential diagnosis between diving related disorders and symptoms related to chemical exposure. These symptoms may overlap making diagnosis difficult. Any individual showing signs or symptoms from exposure or injury should be transported to a hospital for appropriate treatment. Proper documentation on all individuals, methods of decontamination, and any exposures or injuries should be included. Once the individuals leave the medical evaluation area, the decontamination process is complete. The medical treatment after exposure will be conducted in accordance with the specific medical emergency procedures directed by a competent medical team. Again, depending on the type of toxic substance encountered, it may be advisable to introduce short or long term biological and medical surveillance of exposed personnel.

5-5 HAZARDOUS WASTE MINIMIZATION

Federal, state, or local regulations may require that residue collected in the decontamination process be collected and disposed of as hazardous waste. This will require prior coordination with local officials to ensure compliance. Every effort should be made to minimize the amount of waste generated consistent with personnel safety.

APPENDIX A

REFERENCE MATERIALS AND INFORMATION SOURCES

29 CFR 1910-120 Occupational Safety and Health Standards - Hazardous Materials, http://www.osha.gov.

29 CFR 1910 Subpart T Occupational Safety and Health Standards – Commercial Diving Operations, http://www.osha.gov.

Diving in High-Risk Environments 3rd Ed., Steven M. Barsky, Hammerhead Press Santa Barbara, CA http://www.marinemkt.com.

National Institute for Occupational Safety and Health (NIOSH) Pocket Guide to Chemical Hazards contains general industrial hygiene information on several hundred chemicals/classes for workers, employers, and occupational health professionals. http://www.cdc.gov/niosh.

Registry of Toxic Effects of Chemical Substances (RTECS®), Database of toxicological information compiled, maintained, and updated by the National Institute for Occupational Safety and Health. http://grc.ntis.gov/rtecs.htm - subscription fee required.

Chemical and Biological Defense Information Analysis Center (CBIAC) – Information on chemical and biological warfare agents. http://www.cbiac.apgea.army.mil.

U.S. Army Field Manual (FM) 3-9 Potential Military Chemical/Biological Agents and Compounds – available at http://155.217.58.58/atdls.html.

Coast Guard Chemical Hazards Group – maintains the Chemical Hazard Response Information System (CHRIS) database. www.chrismanual.com

Association of Diving Contractors International - www.adc-usa.org.

NOAA Diving Manual, Chapter 13 – Polluted Water Diving available through Best Publication company.
http://www.bestpub.com/

Armed Forces Medical Intelligence Center (AFMIC) Fort Dietrich MD.
https://mic.afmic.detrick.army.mil/.

NOAA Hazardous Materials and Assessment Division – provides tools and information for emergency responders and planners to understand and mitigate the effects of oil and hazardous materials in U.S. waters. http://response.restoration.noaa.gov/

U.S. Environmental Protection Agency
National Health and Environmental Effects Research Laboratory – resource to identify scientific research available on the effects of contaminants on human health. http://www.epa.gov/nheerl/

A-2

This page is left blank intentionally.

www.ingramcontent.com/pod-product-compliance
Lightning Source LLC
Chambersburg PA
CBHW081540280526

45788CB00010B/3306